I Don't Want To Be Homeless:
Trail of a Homeless Man

By Gary Tibbs

xulon PRESS

Copyright © 2004 by Gary Tibbs

I Don't Want To Be Homeless
by Gary Tibbs

Printed in the United States of America

ISBN 1-594673-44-6

All rights reserved by the author. The contents and views expressed in this book are solely those of the author and are not necessarily those of Xulon Press, Inc. The author guarantees this book is original and does not infringe upon any laws or rights, and that this book is not libelous, plagiarized or in any other way illegal. If any portion of this book is fictitious, the author guarantees it does not represent any real event or person in a way that could be deemed libelous. No part of this book may be reproduced in any form without the permission of the author.

Unless otherwise indicated, Bible quotations are taken from the New International Version. Copyright © 1975 by Zondervan Corporation. Published by Harper Collins Publishers, Inc.

Dedication

This book is dedicated to all the homeless and formerly homeless people who are struggling and have struggled through different hardships.

It is also dedicated to: 1) the many social workers and counselors, who go far over and beyond the call of their position; 2) everyone who assists individuals and families in turning their lives around and who helps show people the right direction using their knowledge and resources; 3) those agencies that open not only their doors but their hearts and minds to understand that times are hard if you don't have the skills, education, clothes, food and housing; 4) the programs that help people further their education, to receive their General Educational Development (GED) diplomas, to gain employment skills, life management skills, budgeting finances, anger management, skill builder, home buyers club; 5) those that help with rehabilitation from alcohol and drugs, mental health issues, mental retardation programs, transitional housing, computer training, reunification, shelters, and churches.

Preface

This book is based on facts received from a former homeless man who at one time struggled through life's many challenges. It gives you an out look of how this man, with God's help, was able to break through the invisible wall that kept him on the border line of success. He learned the only way to be able to succeed was to give up what he knew was keeping him down. He speaks clearly on what one needs to do to keep what he or she have received and how to maintain openness for God. He shares some of the tragic moments of his life while living on the street with the day-to-day struggle with alcohol addiction.

Cry of the homeless

I came up in a broken family with no one to really depend on. My father was drunk most of the time, couldn't keep a job, and always pushed my mom around. My mom couldn't help me with my homework because she did not finish school herself and could not read well enough to understand the schoolwork. We were on welfare and could only sometimes make ends meet. I never looked forward to any holidays. I knew there would not be anything for me. I don't want to be homeless.

Gary Tibbs

My teachers did not think that I could learn. They said I was too slow. I never completed my homework because I did not understand how to do it. Now, I am a grown man and still have nothing.

I worked as a handyman at the car wash and held similar jobs that gave me a little pocket change. I even tried janitorial work, but that did not go far because I had to provide a copy of my police clearance and I had been in trouble with the law in the past. I was also expected to provide a urine sample which would have come up dirty. I only smoked a couple of times and only drank when I was lonely, depressed, had some money, or thought about my situation. I guess I'm just like my father. I don't want to be homeless.

Sometimes I try speaking with people to let them know how I'm feeling and the things that are happening to me, but they do not seem to understand. When I tell them about the voices I hear or when I get so down and out and cannot seem to make good decisions, they say everything is going to be all

I Don't Want To Be Homeless

right. But when? I have been living like this so long I don't know any other way. Who is going to help me? Who will spend the time needed to understand me? Why can I not live the way I want, in the woods where I do not have any responsibilities to pay rent, water, or gas? I am okay in the summer when it is nice out.

I cannot face people anyway because I think that they will hurt me. Who is really my friend? Where are you? I don't want to be homeless. Sometimes when people talk to me I do not understand some of the words they use. One person asked me to fill out a job application, but I had to tell them I did not have the time, but if I could take it with me I would bring it back tomorrow. That way, I could get someone else to fill it out for me, and they would never know that I couldn't read. One time, I was trying to fill out a job application and it had a question about my gender. I thought it meant what was my plan. I later found out they were asking what sex I was. I don't want to be homeless.

People always tell me what I need and what is good for me. Could it be they know something I don't? How can I trust them? Why can't they just let me be? I did not ask for your help. Leave me alone. You don't really care about me. I don't want to be homeless.

My Story

I would have never thought that I would become homeless. Yet the streets became my home. Wherever I stopped to rest, that would be my space for the night. There was no hurry to go anywhere, no appointment to keep. Some days were better than others were, if the weather wasn't cold and rainy. Every now and then, I would get a little money by working day labor jobs whenever I could be one of the first in line or could clean up a little. Most places did not want you if you were already dirty before you did the work for them.

When I could not get work for the day, I would get food from soup kitchens, meals on wheels and churches if I could get there on time. I did not have a problem finishing food someone else would leave behind on a table, a park bench, or in the trash can. When you become so hungry that your stomach cramps and you beg for a bag of sugar off the table in a restaurant and no one seems to care, you lose all shame.

I came up in a middle class family with two wonderful and loving parents, two older sisters and one older brother. We were like any other family spending time together having fun. My life started changing when I drank my first beer. I felt as though I was on top of the world and everybody else was looking up to me. I then smoked a little weed and could never stop laughing. It was what was happening. All my friends were doing it, and I thought it was cool.

When I started going to high school, I had lost interest in learning the things one would need to know to be able to make wise choices in life. Two months before graduation, I dropped

I Don't Want To Be Homeless

out of school and went into the military. I would later regret the decision I made. While in the military, it became mandatory for me to go back to school and get my high school diploma. It was not as bad I thought and today I am happy that I received my diploma.

I spent three years in the military and was taught survival skills as well as leadership and respect. The recruiter told me that because I did not have a high school diploma I could only get into the infantry and ride around in tanks. I later found that to be misleading information. I found myself digging many holes that they called one or two men fighting positions. I never rode in or on a tank. We marched everywhere we went. I was not used to camping out in the woods and sometimes we would be out for thirty days or more.

When I left the military, I came back home to live with my parents until I could find a job and a place of my own which did not take long at all. I was twenty-two years old, in my own apartment, had a nice car, and a good job. Yes, this was the life. This is what I had been waiting for, to be able to do my own thing with no restrictions and no curfews. I could stay up all night, leave the TV on, play my music loud, and did not have to answer to anyone. I started going to clubs and hanging out. At first, it was only Friday and Saturday nights. Then it was the whole weekend and then the weekend changed to Wednesday through Sunday.

I started calling in sick or taking emergency leave because I was trying to impress the women that I was meeting. I had women for everyday of the week. I thought it was so cool to be able to hang out. Then it hit me. My bills were not getting paid, I lost my job, and the car dealer wanted full payment or the car. I was given notice to leave my apartment, and I just did not know what to do. The little money I had saved was gone.

My life was crumbling before my eyes. I was too embarrassed to ask my family for help. I turned to my friends but I could not tell them that the big time player who could party all night needed their help. I began to sleep in my car at rest stops and hotel parking lots. I would take showers at the gym after working out until my membership expired. I tried to go back to the military, but they were not taking prior service. I found myself doing odd jobs just to get a couple of dollars for food and gas.

Pride kept me from going to my family for help. I just could not let them see me like this. I began to get so depressed and very lonely. I needed help, but I wanted to get myself out of this mess. The more I thought about what I used to have, the more depressed I became. I started drinking a little beer to help ease the pain. I would start first thing in the morning and drink till the last thing at night. I went thought so many changes from drinking. I did not even remember how I got to a lot of places.

By this time, I had traveled four states from my family. I was glad that they could not see me this way. My car had broken down and I did not have money to get it fixed. It was towed off the street with all that I owned in it. I began to live on the streets begging for food or money. Sometimes I would just hold up a sign. It was like working a full time job. Some people would give and others would not. There were times when someone would stop and hold out a dollar for me to come get it and I would run to get the money. They would drive off laughing and waving the dollar, but I knew everyone was not like that. I just kept going until I had enough for something to eat. There were other times I was given money, and I would get a beer and a small bag of peanuts. Some days I could get a case of beer or some wine.

The alcohol became my food, my friend, and my comforter. I knew I did not look like myself. I could not remember the last time I had brushed my teeth. At one time, I could not stand the smell of my own body. It became very hard to clean up a little. I would use park and service station restrooms if I could find the doors open. Most service stations have their doors locked and they would not give you the key unless you are a paying customer. Some didn't even have soap

I Don't Want To Be Homeless

so you could wash your face and hands. Park restrooms would only be open during the summer season. After a while, I got used to the smell. I even got used to the way people would look at me. I did not have a change of clothes and when I got a chance to clean myself I would wash out my socks and underwear and put them in my pocket or hang them to dry wherever I would stop to rest.

I had lost track of time. It did not make a difference what day it was or what time it was. I would sleep when and where I could or where I felt the safest. I would always stop police officers in the cities I came to and ask for directions to the nearest shelter for a change of clothes or a hot meal. Most shelters were full and did not have space or food. There were many days and nights that I went through without eating.

Trailers were set as shelters in the winter. These were set up for homeless people during the bitter cold nights so we would not freeze to death on the streets. I did not feel safe in them and they smelt awful. But who was I to complain? I was a homeless man, and I was told I should be thankful to have somewhere to sleep. I chose to sleep on the streets. I would put on several layers of clothes that I got from shelters. This practice gave me less to carry, and kept me very warm on those very cold days along with the blankets. I could also keep money I made doing odd jobs. I would put the money in the inner pockets when I had on three or four pair of pants at one time. When I got drunk and passed out, other homeless people went through my belongings. I lost all my identification and that made me feel more depressed.

I had now been on the streets for two years in and out of different shelters in the winter. Most of them would only allow you up to a thirty-day stay. Sometimes you could get lucky and get an extension. You were only given an extension if you were compliant with your service plan which you and your case manager agreed on. You would meet weekly with your case manager and talk about how you became homeless and what you could do to get back on your feet. I knew what I needed to do, but they just never gave me enough time.

It became very frustrating for me. I could not get full time employment without proper identification. It took more than thirty days to receive a copy of my birth certificate and social security card. I could only work labor jobs that paid twenty dollars per day. Even though I wasn't paying rent, I still needed to buy lunch when I worked, and I was still drinking. Every time I met with my case manager, I could feel that this person just did not understand how hard it was for me to get started in the right direction. My case manager was using techniques he learned in school, and I needed more than a weekly meeting and a pep talk.

I did not receive any counseling for my alcohol addiction or depression. The staff did not care if someone abused you or took what few possessions you had. I saw people take shoes, clothes, and money from other guys. I even had clothes and my watch taken from me. I lived in the woods in the summer with other people that I met in shelters. We did not have anyone else that would give us the time of day, but we had each other. I felt very safe and did not need to worry about anyone stealing my belongings.

Everyone had their personal space picked out. We had cardboard linings covered with plastic shaped like tents. We looked out for each other and shared almost everything we received. I lost a lot of weight and had not had a haircut or shave in quite a while. I did not want anyone to recognize me because I was ashamed of what I had become.

Being on the streets at times was hell. Kids and other homeless people beat me. It didn't hurt as much when I was drunk. Sometimes I felt that this was my punishment for all the wrong that I had done to others. I would talk to myself everyday and tell myself to keep going. Sometimes I heard myself speaking out loud. People that would walk by me probably thought I was crazy, but sometimes I needed to hear myself. All I could do then was pray. I needed to get off the streets. I asked God to forgive me, to help me get my life back

I Don't Want To Be Homeless

together, to become a better man, and to stop drinking and using drugs. I always told God that I knew He was watching over me. At least that was what I had been told.

When I stayed in church shelters the people there would always tell me to pray and ask for forgiveness. They always said they would put me in their prayers. I never understood why they were so nice to me. I also remembered when I was growing up my parents had me in church and involved in different programs in the church and learning about Jesus Christ. When I received my first Bible, I was so excited to read and share the word of God as I was developing into a teenager. As I grew up, I had to make decisions in my life. In making those decisions, there were times when I did not want to go to church and sometimes I would go to Sunday school but would not stay for the afternoon service. There were different times, different ways, and different routes that I took.

As I look back, I knew that God wanted me to be a part of His family. As a young man in times of trouble, I always asked

God to put out His hand and help me, to take care of a problem for me, to ease the pain and frustration and make it go away. In the many trials I have had it never dawned on me that there would be a time in my life when I would just sit back and think, a time when I could just look to the sky and ask myself what is it that I could do. I never knew what I wanted to do in life.

I finally realized I wanted to help homeless people. I asked God to direct me in this new found purpose for my life. I had to become homeless myself to be able to understand what their needs were and what they were going through, how they were experiencing homlessness , why they were experiencing it, and how I could best help.

When I tried to explain to individuals I came in contact with and share the things I experienced in my life, they would always say that I did not know what I was talking about, and that I needed documentation of my knowledge and a degree in that area of study. I would have to say that I was an expert because I spent years on the streets learning to survive.

I Don't Want To Be Homeless

People always told me that they knew how I felt and what I was going through, but nobody ever invited me into their homes or helped me to regain full time employment. How could anyone know how I was feeling or even begin to say it is going to be all right? Most of these people had never suffered or had a need or a want for something they could not get. How many of them begged for food or for help to get in out of the cold or just for dry clothes from being soaking wet in the rain all night? How many of them had been thirsty and could not get anything to drink? I had to keep some pride in order to keep going. I knew my family would help me, but I just could not let them see me this way. Which direction should I go? I needed help, but whom could I call on?

Even those who don't believe in God will always speak His name when we are in need or we feel hurt and need comfort. We should always remember that God is always there with every step we take. Why is it that we feel when we ask God to stop the pain and suffering it's supposed to automatically stop?

Who are we to call on God, when we do not honor Him? We always want to receive, but are not willing to give. We as people are like thermometers. We either rise or we fall. Some of us fall and can not get back up. Some of us rise and we forget how we were able to reach the top. Most of us think that all that we have we did ourselves, but we have not done it alone. God has given us all that we have and can take back all that He has given.

When I look back on my life and think of all the trials and tribulations that I went through and all the things I wanted to do in life, I did not realize that I needed to be what God wanted me to be. I never let go until now. I am where God wants me to be and He has fulfilled my dreams and has given me a new life. I lived on the street a total of six years. I was able to get involved with a church shelter for a period of nine months. They provided me with shelter and food. In return, I worked odd jobs around the church and helped family members in the community. I was taught how to care for others and assisted the homeless people that came through the church doors. I would always listen to what they said, their reasons for being homeless, problems they had with drinking, or mental health issues. Some were paranoid and others were very depressed.

I was looking at myself all over again. I wanted so much to find a way to help these people. I was able to save a little money and spoke with the pastor of the church about leaving. I wanted to get closer to my family. He was able to call some of his contacts at other shelters in the area that I was going, and they were willing to give me a job on his recommendation. I asked myself if I was ready to go and could I make a difference for other in need.

The time had come for me to see my family. All I could think of was how they would greet me. Would they understand what I put myself through? Would they still love me and be happy to see me? Walking toward the old neighborhood after getting off the bus I saw that many of the stores had changed.

There were a lot of new faces and a lot of children playing. Many things had changed while I was gone. The closer I came to my parent's house, the more nervous I became. It was a feeling like going in front of the school principal when you knew you had done something wrong. I was acting like a child, and there was no need to act that way. They would either open the door and let me in or they would tell me to go away. I could not believe all the negative things that were going through my mind. I felt like I should just run around and leave. As I was walking up the hill toward the house, I kept repeating to myself that everything was going to be all right.

As I opened the gate to the front yard, I tried my best to keep it from making a sound. Before I could close that gate, my mother had opened the door and all I could see on her face was joy and happiness to see me. She could not wait for me to close the gate fully. She ran to me and gave me a big hug and kiss. She said she knew I was coming home. As I was walking through the front door I could smell the aroma of fresh greens and barbecued ribs, my favorite foods.

My father had been upstairs lying down. He heard my mother screaming "He's here! He's here!" My father came running down the stairs with open arms of joy. He said that my mother told him I would be there today, but he had not given it much thought. He asked how I got there. I told him I rode the subway. He told me that I should have called, and he would have picked me up. I knew that my father was happy to see me. He had me sit down at the dinner table, and my mother asked if I was hungry. I told my mother that after smelling the ribs and greens, she could not stop me from eating. We all sat and ate and no one asked where I had been or what I had been doing. They just talked about all the changes that had taken place since I had been gone.

I knew that sooner or later I would need to tell them where I had been and what I had gone through, but now did not seem to be the right time. I was enjoying being with them and feeling their excitement. Mom asked if I was going to spend the night. I told her no, but that it would be good if she called my brother and sisters and had them come over Saturday so I could tell them about my experiences for the past six years. She agreed and said she would make sure my brother and sisters were there. I did not want to leave, but I needed to get some rest and get ready for work. My father wanted to give me a ride home, but I wanted to take the subway. He insisted on giving me a ride to the subway station, but I told him I wanted to walk.

As I was leaving, I saw some of my old friends that I went to school with and we talked for a while. They were married and had children. We talked about the changes in the neighborhood, and they just assumed I was still in the military. I did not lead them to think anything different. I went on to the subway station. I knew that Saturday would be a good day for me to see everyone again, but I did not know how my brother and sisters would react to hearing about me living on the streets. I could not begin to think of what I would say to make them feel comfortable. I began to pray and ask God to give me the strength and words to speak with my family. I did not know what to expect from them. I knew that my parents would try their best to keep everything under control. During the week, all I could think of was seeing my family and what I would say.

Saturday finally came, and I was ready. I put on a nice pair of jeans and one of my favorite shirts. I wanted to look my best. I was very nervous as I approached the house. I had called my mother during the week to set up a time to be there. She told me to be there at one o'clock. I got there fifteen minutes early so I could feel relaxed, but as I was greeted at the door I saw that my brother and sisters were already there. Mom told me they had been there for about an hour waiting for me. They were just as excited to see me as I was to see them.

Mom had fixed lunch and as we ate, they wanted to know what I had been doing all this time. I told them I had been living on the streets. A silence fell over the room. Everyone was looking at me. My brother started laughing. He told me that was a good one, but for me to tell them the truth. "What have you really been doing?" he asked. As I looked around the room, I saw my oldest sister shaking her head out of disbelief. My mother and father were getting teary eyed. My brother's smile turned into a frown. My other sister's mouth was wide open. I told them that I was homeless and living on the streets until I was able to get the help I needed.

I had done something I thought was impossible for me to do. I had my family speechless. For the first time, my father had nothing to say. My mother said we should all sit down and talk about what I had experienced. I knew my ordeal would leave my family with mixed feelings toward me, but I was determined to let them know what I had been through. I told them that I knew all of them would have done whatever they could to keep me off of the streets, but I felt that I needed to experience being homeless in order for me to know how good I had it and to find myself.

I Don't Want To Be Homeless

"I wanted to call you all and ask for your help," I told them. " But I was dealing with a lot of problems. At the time, I was using drugs and alcohol in order to be cool. I later found myself using them to escape my situation. I was trying to be something I was not. I lost everything, including my job. I was too ashamed to ask for your help. I did not want you to look down on me and I did not want you to feel that I had forgotten all I had learned. I traveled to different states so I would not run across you or my friends. I slept in woods, on bus stop benches, on church steps, in abandoned cars, railroad cars, on the top of apartment building roofs, under bridges, on sidewalks, and in shelters. I felt that all was lost and I would never come back to what I had been before. I met a lot of other homeless people and heard many stories of what they had been through. I had to learn the laws of the street quickly. I learned to respect others that were homeless, what they possess, where they slept, and not to look down on them or think I was better. I did not want to become like some of the people I met. Some talked to themselves and others would do nothing to help themselves because they had given up or had lost hope. I would sometimes pray for peace of mind."

My older sisters asked how I could put my family through the pain of not knowing where I was or what I was doing. I told her that as I looked back at the choice I made, I felt very strongly that I had to work this out myself. I told all of them that I was truly sorry that they all worried about me for so long. Sometimes you never know the road that you are about to travel or the hardships along the way. I could only apologize for how my decision affected them.

My brother told me he would never have thought I would have been homeless. He said we should talk more about my experience sometime. He was just happy to see me. My mother could not even imagine me going through such hard times. She said she had always had a feeling things were not right with me, but she knew that God would show me the way. She was just happy God brought me back home, but asked me to give her my word that if anything like this ever happened again, I would tell the family. My father said I had showed him a side of me he always knew I had. I was the only member of the family to ever go into the military and was always taking on challenges as I grew up. He said he could not expect anything less from me.

My youngest sister just sat speechless with tears running down her face. Not knowing what to make out of this, I asked if she would let me know what she was feeling. After a while, she said she wished I had stayed gone. What is she to think of me eating other people's food and begging for money, living like an animal when I did not need to. She reminded me that I grew up in a middle class family with loving parents and siblings that would have helped at any cost. I had to remind her that as we mature into adults there are many decisions or choices that we face and have to make for ourselves.

"I chose to live on the streets, but I would never do it again with the support I know I have form you all. Pride kept me from coming to my family, but the love that all of you have shown me will keep me here."

She then got up and gave me a hug and told me she still loved me. I was overjoyed and began to cry. I had missed my family and did not want to disconnect from them again. I told them I was renting a room close to my job that I was able to get from helping out in the church.

I started working in a shelter for homeless men and women forty hours a week. It was a start and the money paid the bills; so I could not complain. The only problem I had was working on weekends. I was not able to attend church on Sunday. I thought that by helping others, I would stay on the right track. I would attend church on Tuesday nights and pray sometimes. I started working more hours and on my days off. I made making money my priority. I bought a used car and a motorcycle.

I started hanging out with co-workers at bars and other after hour places. I started climbing the ladder from security monitor to resident manager. I knew if I worked hard I could become a case manager. I really enjoyed working with all the residents, listening to their stories about how they struggled to make ends meet, and telling them of my struggles in life and how I was homeless once myself. I never told them how God became a big part of my life because the director of the shelter was not a Christian, and he did not want any of his staff speaking to the residents about God. I looked forward to going to work everyday because I knew that I made a difference in someone's life.

My day finally came after sharing information on residents to their case workers and other staff. I was able to get information that was needed to help the residents get the services they needed to become self-sufficient. This impressed my boss so much that he offered me a position as a case manager. This was just what I wanted. I made it. I am a case manager. That evening my co-workers and I got together and celebrated. I took all the credit for making it to the next level.

I started off with a caseload of five that soon became

twenty-five. There was no stopping me now. I wanted to help as many people as I could. The substance abuse counselor distracted me every time she walked by my desk. She was very pretty and spoke with authority. She would speak about drinking and drugs to the residents. I wanted to learn more about alcohol and its effect on the body. I also wanted to get to know her. We had lunch a few times, went out, and became close. I learned so much from her about drugs and alcohol. I attended workshops and took classes to become a certified addiction counselor (CAC). I learned that she was a heavy drinker as well.

I found myself getting more and more involved with the things that started my homelessness. Here I was drinking again wildly. I was involved with a woman who could not wait until it was time to get off work to have that first drink. This was not at all the kind of relationship I was looking for. I was going backward. I did not need or want this. I stopped going to church, stopped praying, and forgot who put me back on the right track. I needed help and direction, but I could not find the strength to pull myself out. I was once again on a path that led nowhere. I moved in with her to help with the bills and be closer to work. At least that is what I told myself. I was working, but my feelings for others seemed to be gone. I would work fine with the residents of the shelter, but could not get along with the staff. I had to stop hanging out with co-workers because I did not want them to see me getting so drunk that I could barely walk.

Every night, I would drink myself to sleep. I would wake up in the morning on the cot, my bed, or sometimes on the floor. I was very luck to avoid getting arrested for drunk driving, especially on bowling nights. I must have drunk at least four pitchers plus the bottles I would have in my bowling bag. I had hurt so many people in my life that meant well because of my attitude and what I had become. I had shut down from my friends. I only hung around people that got drunk, and every activity I was involved in consisted of being able to get drunk.

Then it happened, the day that I had not planned for. We had been drinking very heavily and one thing led to another. I disagreed with her about rehab programs. The argument started and there was a lot of name-calling. She started crying and pushing me and telling me to get out. I just went into the bedroom and shut the door behind me. I had had enough. Next thing I remember was the police coming in the bedroom asking me what was happening. I told them nothing, just a little disagreement. The officer asked me why I hit her. I told him that I had not put my hands on her. The next thing I remember, they were putting me in handcuffs and escorting me out of the house. I spent two hours in jail and was released on my own recognizance. She was waiting for me in the lobby. She told me how sorry she was for putting me through a sharking ordeal. I was speechless. I felt betrayed, empty, and lost. Who was this person that I had gotten involved with? Why did this happen? Did she have any feeling of hurt or shame for this type of action? I did not know what to do.

I Don't Want To Be Homeless

The only thing she could say was "Let's go home." I did not want to go, but I had no other options. Something kept telling me to get out, but I kept telling myself it was going to be all right. I knew that I was lying to myself, but I did not want to think or hear anything different. I knew it was wrong for me to be living with her. I also knew it was wrong for me to be physically involved without being married. I kept telling myself to leave, but the alcohol kept telling me to stay. I needed help and was too ashamed to ask for it. I was helping everybody else with his or her problems, but could not help myself.

As time went by, there were more and more problems, arguments, blaming, and fighting. This went on for over a year. I woke up every morning saying to myself that I was going to change. I wanted so much to get my life together and I began to pray and ask God to forgive me and help me get out of the situation. I knew that God heard me, but I did not think that He would help me. I had called on God so many times and time after time God would give me the direction to go and I would screw it up. I guess I was thinking that maybe God was tired of coming to my aid.

I took a good look at myself in the mirror, and I did not like what I saw. I was out of shape. I had lost the clean-cut look that I had regained when I was not using alcohol. I started jogging every morning and working out at the gym in order to regain self-confidence, but I was still drinking myself to sleep. I could fool everyone around me, but I could not fool myself. I was a closet alcoholic. I did not have anyone to talk to about my problems. I did not make time in my everyday schedule to attend Alcoholics Anonymous meetings.

I decided to handle this problem on my own. I told myself that I could solve this drinking problem. I even convinced myself that I had cut down on heavy drinking. I was feeling good about myself, but the only person I was fooling was myself. I had distanced myself from people who wanted to get close to me. I was afraid that they would see I had a problem with alcohol.

I Don't Want To Be Homeless

I was doing find with keeping people far away from me until she appeared. Her hair was as red as autumn leaves. She had a scent of fresh flowers in a garden. Her smile was like the calm of an ocean. Her beauty was as snowflakes falling from the sky. She had come to the facility to volunteer. She was going around meeting the staff when I saw her. She said, "Hello, my name is Dee." She had watched me interact with the residents at the facility and thought it was remarkable how I could ease their minds and help them solve their problems. She told me that I had a good rapport with the residents. She wanted to know how I was led to working with homeless people. I told her a lie. I thought that if she knew I had traveled the same road as most of the people here she would look at me differently. We began to talk a lot about goals we had set to accomplish. What we had done and where we were going.

She was in school studying to be an engineer and had two children in school. She also stated that she was a Christian. I told her I had been in the military and wanted to make a difference in someone's life. I told her I was a Christian, but had fallen. She just smiled and said she would pray for me. We had lunch a few times and even dinner. We were building a great friendship, and I was always able to keep my drinking under control while I was in her presence. As I grew closer to her, I started revealing to her that I had a problem with alcohol by my actions. She took notice to my alcohol use and offered to help, but I was closed to discussion.

I let her know I was living with someone, and it was not good. I told her I wanted to move out, but I had a lot of fears. I wanted help, but I did not know what I would do if I stopped drinking. All my friends drank and all my social activities consisted of having a drink. She always told me to pray.

I went to church with her one Sunday, and it was just what I needed in order to know that God had never left me. I was beginning to find myself again. We had grown very fond of each other. She told me I needed to move away from where I was living. Through her I found strength. I was ready to let my girlfriend know that I was moving out. When I arrived home, she was there. She had been drinking, but I did not think that much about it. I wanted to wait until the next day to tell her I was moving out, but I did not want to put it off any longer and change my mind. I told her I was moving in the morning. She became very angry and told me all I did was use her and I was not going to get away without paying for it. She threw glasses and picked up a chair, and I ran out of the house without anything. I did not want any trouble. As I left, she shouted that she was going to call the police.

I went to the nearest telephone and called Dee and explained what happened. She told me to stay put and not to return to the house. When she arrived she told me it was going to be all right and that I could stay in her guestroom for the night. That morning we both went to the police station and sure enough they had a warrant for my arrest. I was released in a couple of hours, and I had the police escort me to my ex-girlfriend's home to retrieve my belongings.

I went to court and saw the same judge. He dropped the charges and ordered her to get an evaluation. Once again, God had prevailed. I found myself getting more and more involved with my Christian friend. I was falling in love. She told me many times how much she loved me and time after time I acted as if it did not matter. I knew that I could not keep her happy. I did not know if I would ever get my drinking under control. I thought that she was too good for me and I did not want to be a burden in her life. She was going to the top and I would have just been in the way. I wanted the best for her. She needed a God fearing Christian man and I knew that I was not the guy. She had talked to me about getting involved in a rehabilitation program for alcoholics. I found a program that was ninety days long.

I spoke with my boss about the rehab program, and he was very surprised to learn that I had a drinking problem. He said I was the last person he would ever think had any problems. It was a big step for me to even speak about it. I told him that I

I Don't Want To Be Homeless

wanted to keep my job if it was possible. He explained that in the employee policy I was covered and I could use my sick leave. Now, I would need to take care of my rent for three months while I was going through treatment. Dee said she would collect all my mail and give the landlord my rent payments each month. I was ready to go.

Dee took me to the treatment center and dropped me off. I thought that I would really miss her, but this was something I had to do. I was tired of getting drunk everyday, waking up with headaches, and not knowing how many people I had hurt with words and insults. I wanted to leave within three days. I was so afraid of getting to know myself. I constantly spoke with the counselors to get an uplift that everything was going to be all right. I told him I was not a quitter. I would stay in this program, but I kept thinking about having a drink. After being there for the first thirty days, I started regaining my feeling. The substance abuse counselor told me that I needed to have at least one year of clean time before I thought of getting involved in a relationship. I needed very much to get to know myself and what I had become and who I wanted to be.

I did not call Dee much from the treatment center. I was working on staying clean and staying focused. After being clean for two months, I was back into praying daily and reading my Bible. I was feeling that this time around was it. I was starting to count the days left. On one hand, I was afraid to leave, but on the other hand I wanted to get back to work. I knew that I would not be able to get into a serious relationship until I was able to stay off alcohol. I did not need any other responsibilities at this time. Trying to stay clean was a responsibility in itself. How was I going to explain this to Dee?

Would she understand what needed to come first in my life in order for me to make things possible to have a life? Would she think that I just used her or that I did not care how it would affect her? All I could do was pray about it and hope that this would not hurt our friendship.

Then the day came for me to leave. I had been clean for

ninety days. I felt good, looked good, and I had learned something about myself that I was not aware of. I did not need alcohol to find peace in my life. While in treatment, I received weekly counseling. I did not realize that I had so many bitter feelings inside of me. A lot of things happened in my childhood that came out during these sessions. I cried many nights like a baby. I was regaining my feelings. I was told that the alcohol made my feelings numb. I had to learn who I was and how to control my feelings. I realized that I could never drink alcohol again, but that was all right with me. I had let this thing beat me down enough. I, with God's help, was ready to move forward and live an alcohol-free life.

Dee was there to pick me up and it was so nice to see her. Her smile alone made me realize that she was pleased that I completed the ninety-day program. We talked about how things were going and how I was feeling. I knew that we needed to talk about where I was going and what I was told regarding being involved with someone, but I could not find the right moment to start telling her what I needed to do. I did not want to hurt her, but deep down inside I already had. I wanted so badly to tell her how much I loved her and how she had always been there for me. Whenever I needed to talk, she would stop whatever she was doing and talk to me. When I needed someone to hold, she was there for me. When I was depressed, she could make me feel so special. She even wanted to attend the AA meetings with me. I knew that she was a good woman, but I still needed to get myself together.

I did not know how to tell her that I needed time for myself so I stopped calling her and did not return her calls. I would not open the door to let her in. By this time eleven months had gone by, and I finally called her. She let me know that she had been waiting and I never called or wrote to let her know what was happening with me. As a result, she began to date a man that she met through a friend. She told me all I had needed to do was call and she would have understood. I did not realize that she was God-sent until it was too late.

I Don't Want To Be Homeless

The only thing I could do was think of how foolish I had been. I had lost the only person that I had ever loved. I wanted to be her friend but we agreed that it would not work out. I wanted to get away and let wounds heal from feelings of respect and love of a person I admired. I have since moved on with my life and was able to find full time work in another state. I went back to school to further my knowledge in the areas of counseling and motivation. There have been many times that the thought of drinking has come up, but I lost so much at different times that I did not want to lose what I had regained. My faith in God has opened many doors in my life and God has given me direction and the ability to recognize what I need and what I don't. I cannot take back the hurt and pain I have caused others nor can I get back everything I lost. I can only say that we all have a purpose in life and I had to experience hard times in order to find who I was to become. God was the answer for me. He could be your answer as well.

Open Your Heart

A lot of us do not understand how so many people can become homeless. So many of us feel that homeless people are lazy and do not want to work. Others think homeless people just want the government to take care of them. Anyone can become homeless through loss of employment, loss of a loved one, spousal abuse, drug and alcohol abuse, mental health issues, lack of education, lack of skills, inability to budget (time /money /needs/ wants), physical challenges, lack of enough income (high debts, child support payments, rent, transportation).

When we see a homeless person on the streets holding up a sign (homeless will work for food or money), what is really going through your mind? Do you ask yourself if the person is really homeless and needs help? Have you ever asked yourself, "Suppose that was me"? Some of us think that homelessness is a disease we can catch. Is that why we do not allow shelters and group homes or any other facilities in our communities? In some states shelters and group homes are only allowed in industrial areas. What does it take for us to help our fellow man or woman? When you see a homeless person, can you have empathy for that person?

Some people are on the streets because of a learning disorder (L D). You can teach them for years, but they can only retain so much. Sometimes they forget even the smallest of things like washing their face or tying their shoes. Throughout their life they are on the borderline. They want to do so much, but are very limited.

We have physically challenged individuals, some who had

I Don't Want To Be Homeless

worked at one time, now having an injury that affects their ability to work. They apply for unemployment and receive it, but after a few months it runs out. They try to get into some type of training program to learn a trade that they can perform in spite of their disability. They are informed there are no openings for six months to a year. They apply for social security and get turned down. All this time there is no income available, no family in the area, or their family has no space to move them into their home. The homeless person goes into a shelter and one year later they receive benefits, but not enough to pay the rent, buy food, and use public transportation.

We see people talking to themselves, fighting an imaginary person, or using foul language. It may appear that they are looking in your direction. They could be suffering from schizophrenia. Some of the symptoms of schizophrenia are delusion, grossly disorganized or catatonic behavior, hallucinations, and disorganized speech. There are also different mood disorders that keep people from functioning or living what some of us consider a normal life.

We think that most of the people that are homeless have problems with drugs. Some self medicate with drugs because they do not want to face the reality of the life they are living. Some have lost hope and have given up on themselves. Others do not like the side effects or changes that prescribed drugs cause. This keeps them from getting the professional help they need to maintain stability.

Why is it that people always compare themselves to others, especially when someone is down? Have you ever heard yourself say, "If I can do it, you can?" We fail to realize that our minds function differently. We may read the same article from a paper but interpret the message differently. With a variety of up bringing, schools, and styles of instruction, education, discipline and belief, we look at each situation differently. You do not need to like someone to work with them. We need to learn how to work together, regardless of our differences.

"If anyone has material possessions and sees his brother in

need but has no pity on him, how can the love of God be in him? Let us not love with words or tongue but with actions and in truth." I John 3:17-18

Printed in the United States
21390LVS00001B/181-204